6 Figures Blogging Blueprint

A Step-By-Step Guide To Sky Rocket Your Fame and Earnings FAST!

By

Adrian D'Luca

Copyright © 2020 by Sentral Specks Publishing

All Rights Reserved. No part of this book or any of its contents may be reproduced, copied, modified, distributed, stored, transmitted in any way form or by any means, or adapted the prior written consent of the author.

This book is licensed for the purchaser's enjoyment only. This e-book may not be resold or given away to other people. If you would like to share a copy of this book, please purchase an extra copy for each individual. If you are reading this book and did not purchase it, or it was not purchased for your use only, then please buy your copy to enjoy. Thank you for respecting the hard work put into the making of this book.

www.getpublishedinthreedays.com

Table of Contents

INTRODUCTION 5
CHAPTER 1 6
BLOGGING 6
   What's a blog? 6
      Blog vs. Website: What's the difference? 6
   The Types and Purposes of Blogs 7
      Personal Blog 7
      Personal Brand Blog 7
      Business Blog 7
      Niche Blog 8
      Affiliate Blog 8
CHAPTER 2 10
4 STEPS TO STARTING YOUR BLOG 10
   #Step 1– Goals: What does Successful Blogging mean to you? 10
      Traffic 10
      Personal Satisfaction 10
      Comments and Engagements 10
      Economic Empowerment 10
      Other Results 11
   # Step 2– Choosing a message 11
      Choose a Topic that you're genuinely interested in 11
      Choose a Topic for which you're likely to find an audience 11
   #Step 3: Finding your audience 13
      Google 13
      Quora 14
      Pinterest 14
      Facebook Groups 14
   # Step 4 Setting Up your blog 15
      Choosing a Name 15
      Launching your blog on the Web 15
CHAPTER 3 16
PROMOTING YOUR BLOG AND BUILDING YOUR COMMUNITY 16

- A. USING SOCIAL MEDIA 16
  - Determine which Social Networks to Use 16
  - Know Where Your Target Readers Are 16
  - Find Out the Networks that Promise Huge Traffic 16
  - Make Sharing Easy By Integrating Social Media with Your Blog 17
  - Place a Link to Your Blog in Your Social Media profiles 17
  - Re-share Older Content 18
  - USING DIFFERENT SOCIAL MEDIA SITES TO PROMOTE YOUR BLOG 18
- B. BUILDING YOUR MAILING LIST 21
  - Getting subscribers 21
- C. USING SEARCH ENGINE OPTIMIZATION 22
  - On-Site SEO Measures 22
  - Off-Site SEO Measures 24

CHAPTER 4 25
MONETIZING YOUR BLOG 25
- MAKING A GOOD IMPRESSION AND MAKING YOURSELF ACCESSIBLE 25
  - About Page 25
  - Partnership Page 25
  - Contact Page 26
- PRICING YOURSELF 26
  - Pricing Based on Activity Type 27
- EARNING OPPORTUNITIES 27
  - Advertising 27
  - Affiliate Marketing 29
  - Products and Subscriptions 29
  - Sponsored Blog Posts 30
  - Other Earning Opportunities 30
- CONCLUSION 32

INTRODUCTION

We owe the internet so much. Because of it, we can connect with others seamlessly, broaden our horizons and enjoy the spectacles of places we haven't visited physically. But that's not all. Some people also owe the wealth they have accumulated to this global connection of computer networks (yes, big Jeff is one of them). With the countless opportunities available, these people have seized some and made a fortune out of them. And you can join that class by taking blogging seriously. No kidding.

Several bloggers bag six-figure incomes almost effortlessly from their adventures behind a computer screen. With a mixture of skill and grit, they are steadily living the good life. And that should be your target too. However, for this journey, you'd need a guide, and this book will serve that purpose without fail. Embedded in its confines are practical tips and insights you can use in building a blog from scratch and promoting it aggressively. You'll also learn the earning opportunities available to you as a blogger and how to snap them up intentionally. Wondering how you can get advertisers and brands to partner with you? We have that and many other things covered too. So delve in and arm yourself with all you need to make six-figures as a blogger.

CHAPTER 1
BLOGGING

Blogs have become quite intricately woven to the fabric of the society- or at least the online society. As of 2019, there were about 600million registered blogs on the internet, according to *Growth Badger*. You'd think that for something so popular, everyone would be able to define it. But that's not the case. Some people couldn't even identify a blog if it spat at them in the face. The likely reason for this is that there isn't one universally accepted definition of what a blog is. So in this report, rather than just give you one (or many) definition(s) of a blog is alone, I'll also focus on the essence of what makes a blog a blog.

What's a blog?
Etymologically speaking, the word "blog" is derived from the amalgam of the words "web" and "log." In fact, from the early 90s, the naming of this popular 21st-century digital entity went through quite a bit of metamorphosis. First, it was referred to as "weblog." It later morphed into "we blog" before the word "blog" finally stuck.

Blogs grew out of online journals, which were fast becoming rampant in the mid-90s. As the internet grew, many internet users started to run personal webpages where they published general information about their lives and their views about happenings in the world around them. Even today, several years deep into the 21st century, blogs still serve this function. So, you may think of a blog as an online equivalent of a traditional diary. Like a traditional journal or diary, a typical blog is written in informal language, the kind of language that characterizes day to day personal communication. An important clarification here: It isn't just individuals who run blogs. Businesses and corporations own and run blogs too. Later, we will discuss different types of blogs, their purposes, and their benefits but suffice it to say for now that all blogs are not created equal.

Blog vs. Website: What's the difference?
Although every blog is a type of website, not every website is a blog. Unlike a typical website, a blog contains frequently updated information that is arranged in reverse chronological order, so that information shown on the site ranks from the most recent to the least recent. This feature is a major distinguishing characteristic between a blog and a website. Whereas most websites are updated only occasionally, some blogs update their content even multiple times per day. You may also wonder which one is better; a blog or a website. The answer to that query is determined by what you aim to achieve with your site.

Summarily, a blog is a frequently updated informational website, characterized by posts that are arranged in reverse chronological order. Two other features common to a blog but absent on a website are the *comments* feature and *social sharing* icons. The comment feature allows a visitor to leave a comment on a blog posting while the social sharing icons allow the blog audience to share any blog post on their desired social media platforms.

The Types and Purposes of Blogs

For many individuals, blogging remains a form of public, online journal. But the question remains, *"why are many more people choosing to go public with their thoughts and opinions?"* One obvious benefit is that thanks to several technological advancements and modifications, it is now

> **6 Figure$ Tip**
> *The purpose of your blog sets the tone for the structure of your blog.*

possible to make bank just by owning a blog. Perhaps, the goal of reaping a harvest of huge dollars is the reason you've picked up this report. Nonetheless, beyond making money, there are many underlying reasons why people blog. When you know the different types of blogs that exist and the diverse purposes they serve, it guides you in structuring your blog to achieve your predetermined intentions.

Personal Blog

Just as implied by the name, this kind of blog is focused on the blogger. These blogs have stuck entirely to the purpose blogs originally served. A personal blog is poised to communicate anything and everything that interests the blog owner. The blogger writes about his hobbies, beliefs, interests, feelings, experiences, and even frustrations. The success of the blog depends on whether or not the blog owner can find other people whose thoughts resonate with his. From there on, a community is built. It's important to know that the content of a personal blog is not niche-specific. The blogger may write about anything that pleases him.

Personal Brand Blog

People often run blogs as part of their branding endeavors. Personal branding, by the way, refers to the coordinated and intentional efforts of creating a brand around a person. The individual makes conscious efforts to market her skills and abilities and cause the public to perceive her as an authority in her field. The process of personal branding involves employing all the tools that a business would use when building a brand, including a website, social media, and of course, a blog. A personal brand blog is similar to the personal blog in that they both have a lot to do with the blog owner. But, while the personal blog has a myriad of subjects he can write about, the personal brand as narrowed his focus to a fewer number of subjects. The goal of a personal brand blogger is to establish herself as a thought leader in the field where she writes. A few brilliant examples of a personal brand are the personal brands of Kylie Jenner- the billionaire girl of the Kardashian family, and Gary Vaynerchuk, an American-Belarusian entrepreneur.

Business Blog

Many businesses that own websites have also built dedicated blogs as part of their overall marketing strategy. There are many benefits to this decision. When a business runs a well SEO optimized blog, it helps them generate more organic leads to their website. The approach to a business blog is to write on topics that have worth to their ideal clients. More savvy businesses even go as far as giving *freemiums*. A *freemium* is a piece of information so valuable that the prospective client would be happy to pay for it, but it is given out for free. An ever-flowing stream of relevant information, in turn, allows a business to build trust and nurture its relationship with its audience. Doling out high-quality content is only the first step. The idea is to convert these visitors to leads and, through a series of processes, convert them into paying customers.

Niche Blog
Niche blogs are highly specific blogs. Rather than dabble into a broad range of topics, a niche blog tapers down the options and focuses on it. Examples of niche ideas are home décor blogging, parenting blogging, fashion blogging, religious blogging, lifestyle blogging, food blogging, etc. Some blogs get even narrow into the niches and concentrate on a small segment of a larger niche. An example of this would be a seafood blog. The overarching niche is food, but then, this blog focuses exclusively on edible sea creatures.

There's a similarity between a personal brand blog and a niche blog. They are both tailored to a niche market. There's a major difference, though. While the personal brand blog is built around the blogger, discussions on the niche blog are focused more on the niche itself. When choosing a niche, it is vital to pick a topic that you find fascinating. It's also important to ensure that your niche market is going to attract enough people. Your success as a blogger is hinged upon how much traffic you have on your site. As such, a niche in a topic that doesn't appeal to a massive number of internet users is to see your business up for failure.

Affiliate Blog
Affiliate bloggers review products that are produced by other businesses. They produce content that encourages visitors on their blog to purchase a product. When a web user purchases a product using any of the affiliate links on the blogger's site, the blogger earns a commission. Success in affiliate blogging requires a lot of SEO efforts since web users are only going to be engaging links that they can see.

Foundationally, these are five primary types of blogs that exist. Keep in mind that a blog may, however, overlap in their functions and their models. For instance, a personal blog could as well be an affiliate blog.

You have seen that a blog can serve many purposes. Some use it just simply to exercise their artistic muscles and showcase their creativity and talents, some use it to establish themselves as authorities in their industry, some also use it just to connect and socialize with other fellow hobbyists or persons with similar values and interests. And many businesses likewise have found a way to cash-in on the benefits that a blog provides. They now incorporate it in their marketing strategies and use them as a channel for lead generation and, ultimately, customer acquisition. To determine which sort of blog is perfect for you, simply take a step back and picture the goals you want to accomplish in the long-term. Your goals will be your guide.

CHAPTER 2
4 STEPS TO STARTING YOUR BLOG

Setting up a blog is incredibly easy. Thanks to platforms like WordPress, Blogger Medium, and so on, with a few clicks, without coding skills and without making any down payment, you can have your blog up and running. That is likely why there's been an increasing number of blogs today. Again, setting up a blog has become a no-brainer. However, building a successful blog is no simple task. There steps to follow to set up a blog that will thrive, reach a huge audience, and hopefully (if it's your goal) become a source of your economic empowerment. I have summarized them into 4 steps altogether. Following these 4 steps will greatly increase your chances of success in starting and running your blog.

#Step 1– Goals: What does Successful Blogging mean to you?
The best place to start your journey to becoming a six-figure blogger is by defining what success in blogging means to you as a person. Since different people have varied reasons for blogging, success in blogging means differently to different people. In my experience, though, any of these are the 5 indicators of success common to most, if not all, blogs.

Traffic
Virtually every blogger hopes to attract a large audience to their blog. Otherwise, they could have written for an audience of one. That's why it is often commonplace for a blogger to be concerned about the amount of daily traffic attracted by his or her blog.

Personal Satisfaction
The prospect of sharing one's thoughts, showcasing one's talents, and creative genius to a public audience is found to be thrilling to some people.

Comments and Engagements
Some bloggers derive huge satisfaction in seeing other web users engage their posts in some way, either by commenting on the posts, *liking* the posts, or sharing it. This is common amongst hobbyist-type bloggers.

Economic Empowerment
Here comes the obvious one. Many people are, in fact, in this for the money. If you can turn a hobby into a source of income, having fun and making money while at it, why not do so? Not everyone thinks this way, though! A recent and popular example of a fellow who did not go into blogging for the money is a person named the guy who turned don advertiser money for his high traffic COVID-19 website.

Other Results

Other goals could include selling a product, raising money for a public cause, establishing thought leadership, and whatnots.

Before you start your blog, you must think through what successful blogging looks like for you. Remember the proverbial saying about climbing to the top of the ladder of success only to find out it as leaning against the wrong wall? You don't want to waste effort and labor only to realize that the *kind of success* you've got isn't the *kind of success* you wanted.

Step 2- Choosing a message

There are countless numbers of topics you could blog about, and you have absolute liberty on what topic you choose. You could use your blog to share your expertise in an area of proficiency, covering celebrity gossip, talk national or international politics, or whatever it is you desire. The problem for most to-be bloggers isn't the ability to find a topic to blog about. On the contrary, it is selecting from the millions of options available. The options of the topic you could blog on are so numerous that you could easily be inundated while trying to make a decision.

Fortunately, you don't have to get it right the first time. You are safe to jump into this water and wade your way through to clarity. Although ironic, you're less likely to drown by jumping in this water body than you are to drown by standing at the seashore. Like Billionaire entrepreneur Mark Zuckerberg said, *"Ideas don't come out fully formed. They only become clearer as you work on them"*. You are certainly going to be better off starting even when a bit of fuzziness still exists around your thoughts. As you progress and learn and iterate, you will see your ideas get clearer. That said, there are two basic tips to serve as a guide when choosing your topic;

> **6 Figure$**
> **Tip** *If you start your blogging journey with clear goals, everything you do from here will be easier.*

Choose a Topic that you're genuinely interested in.
I'll share a list of 80 most recommended topics shortly to blog about. But this list is meant to serve only as a guide. Blogging (like any type of work) should be fun, and your desire to make money out of it shouldn't push you to compromise on that. If you aren't intensely passionate about the niche you are blogging in, that which was meant to be a rollercoaster ride would quickly be reduced to a slogging through. More so, if you're not passionate about the subject you're writing about, your audience will likely see that, and they'll walk away from you. Both ways, you lose.

Choose a Topic for which you're likely to find an audience.
This tip is more important, especially when you're blogging for money. When streamlining your options of blog topics, consider which options are most likely to gain traction has merit with an audience. The natural human tendency is wishful thinking. You have to be rigorous on your self-

analysis and, as much as possible, select a topic that is not only a hobby for you but would be found interesting by a large number of people.

80 Most Profitable Blog Niches

Market research has proven that the following niche markets have the highest traction in the blogging universe

1. Personal Fitness
2. Health and Fitness
3. Food
4. Beauty and Fashion
5. Special Education
6. Homesteading
7. Survival Planning
8. Real Estate Investment Education
9. Organization
10. Home Décor
11. Gardening
12. Crafts
13. Personal Development
14. Travel
15. Pet Care
16. Writing
17. Art for Educators
18. Freelance Business
19. DIY Upholstery for Automobiles
20. Parenting
21. Sewing
22. Frugal Living
23. Christian Living
24. Video Games Review
25. App Reviews
26. E-commerce
27. Newborn
28. Tech Gadget Reviews
29. Photography
30. Relationship Advice
31. Painting
32. Photoshop Tutorials
33. Learning a Language
34. Hand Lettering
35. Trading Stocks
36. Web Development
37. Virtual Reality
38. Vegan Cooking
39. Psychology
40. Audio Production
41. Building websites
42. Travel Photography
43. Men's Lifestyle
44. Body Building
45. Yoga
46. Learning New Skills
47. Astronomy and Space
48. Personal Style
49. Family Life
50. Video game Strategies
51. Marathon Running
52. Hiking trials
53. Copywriting
54. Software development
55. Video Editing
56. Eco Lifestyle
57. Golf Tutorials
58. Productivity tips
59. Marathon Running
60. Home Cooking

61. Cryptocurrency
62. Asian Food Recipes
63. Gaming
64. Drawing
65. Restaurant Reviews
66. Scuba Diving
67. Self-defense training
68. Interior design
69. Car repairs
70. Cars
71. Sustainable Living
72. College Planning
73. Business Consulting
74. Dating Advice
75. Organic Food recipes
76. Art & Culture
77. Fishing
78. Book Reviews
79. Healthy Food Recipes
80. Web Design

#Step 3: Finding your audience

Your target audiences are the set of people who your content is most likely to help. The more accurately you can describe your audience (who they are and what they need), the faster you are to succeed as a blogger. For one thing, you will produce more superior content. The superiority of content is not referring to the gravitas with which you convey your thoughts. Rather, it's referring to you delivering precise solutions and answers to the problems and questions your audience is facing. Since you're delivering content that they find relevant to their needs, guess what, they'll keep coming back. In other words, you are begging to grow a fan base- and audience of loyal customers.

> **6 Figure$ Tip**
> *A successful blog is born when you find the sweet spot between your area of interest and a need in the market.*

Once you have a considerably large number of loyal customers, everything else works almost seamlessly. A loyal following of people act as ambassadors for your blog, causing it to go viral. Selling any products to a loyal audience is easier. As you engage your audience via comments and your blogs, social media platforms, generating content ideas would also be easier. Having seen the many benefits of precisely defining your target audience, the question to ask is, "how do you find your blog target audience?"

Remember that the ultimate goal is to be able to describe your ideal visitor or in marketing terminology, create your target audience persona. Put differently, you want to know what is going on in the mind of your ideal blog audience so that you can more fiercely, pointedly, but subtly address their challenges. The way to determine this information to look for hints on platforms that your target audience is already frequenting. Here are a few of such platforms.

Google

This is the quickest and most obvious way to identify your ideal audience. Start off by initiating a query related to your blog niche. As soon as you have typed out a few words in your search engine, Google suggests some topics based on common related questions that it has had to respond to. Also, upon fully completing your search, you will find at the end of the search results, a list of "related searches" listed by Google These suggestions are hints into what our target audience is reading.

Quora
Quora can be described as a question and answer platform. As such, it's a great place to find out that questions people are currently asking about your blog niche. First, do a few searches on some topics in your blog niche. When the search results appear, you will see the "related questions" section on the right-hand side of your screen. These questions will give you insights into what people are talking about.

Pinterest
Pinterest works a lot like the Google search engine. When you enter a keyword, Pinterest suggests keywords relevant to your query.

Facebook Groups
Although Facebook communities are not exactly the bustling space they once were, they are still a great place to get a clue on what it is that matters to people in a niche audience. Search for public groups built around your blog niche. By looking at the content shared on these groups, querying them, and cross-referencing them against your findings on the other platforms, you'll have insights into the questions that matter to your clients.

> **6 FigureS Tip**
> *As a blog-preneur, more than anything else, you must know your market and you must be able to decrypt what their wants are.*

Competitor Blogs

There's nothing wrong with looking to other blogs for ideas as long as you're not doing so to become a copycat. What you should do instead is pay attention to which posts are performing well for them, information that they may have left out that you may add in your posting. Resist the temptation import content from competitor websites directly. There's probably no faster way to damage your reputation as a blogger.

As a blog-preneur, it's first and foremost your responsibility to know as much as you can about the audience you aim to serve. The more you relate with and understand your target audience, the better positioned you are to produce content that they will fall in love with. This knowledge is pivotal to the success of your blog, and the only way to know is to keep your ears to the ground.

Step 4 Setting Up your blog

At this stage, you have come to the end of the pre-planning operations. You've chosen your topic/niche, defined your target audience persona, and researched competitor sites to investigate underserved needs that your blog can serve. It's time for you to get the show on the road.

Choosing a Name

Choosing a name that you feel secure about is often a tough decision for bloggers to make. You may find yourself having sleepless nights over it. The truth sometimes, we place a disproportionate amount of significance on the name of the blog. It is an important decision, no doubt. But it isn't all-important! When choosing your blog name, make sure that it is;

- Descriptive- that is, it tells a first-time reader something about what your blog represents
- Easy to Spell and Remember.
- Unique.

Launching your blog on the Web

Hosting your blog is the process that makes your blog visible on the Web. There are 3 decisions you need to make at this stage.

> **6 Figure$ Tip**
> *For a seamless entry into the blogosphere, choose WordPress as your software provider.*

1. *Your Domain name.*

Your domain name is what type into their browsers to visit your blog. For instance, the domain name for Google is *www.google.com*. You may think of it as your blog's address on the Web. Ideally, your domain name should simply be your blog name followed by an extension such as .com, .co, .org, .net, and so forth. You'd have to do a domain search to ensure that whatever domain name you have in mind hasn't already been taken by some other web user.

2. *Your blogging software provider*

You need a software provider to write your blog. Like a word processor, blogging software is a program that you'll use to create and manage your blog. Several blogging software products exist chief of which is the WordPress software. *WordPress provides software for approximately 60% of websites on the internet today.* Other popular software providers are Wix, Joomla, Drupal, Shopify, Magneto, and Squarespace.

3. *Your hosting provider*

You may think of your hosting provider as your landlord. They provide you with accommodation on the World Wide Web. Hence the name- a *hosting* provider. There are several popular options to choose from- Bluehost (the industry leader), HostGator, DreamHost, GoDaddy, SiteGround, Cloudways, A2Hosting, GreenGeeks, iPage, and a host of others. With less than $3 a month, you'll have your blog hosted.

Once this is settled, all that's left is to design the aesthetics of your blog. Afterward, get the blogging going.

CHAPTER 3
PROMOTING YOUR BLOG AND BUILDING YOUR COMMUNITY

A. USING SOCIAL MEDIA

Social media provides a great way for you to promote your blog and generate more traffic. And you know that translates to vaster opportunities to make more money as you target that six-figure mark. But cross-promoting your content on social media – as most bloggers discover in the long run – is far beyond just sharing links to your blog posts on a gazillion platforms. And sorry, having great content alone won't do too. There's no magic wand you can wave to have millions of social media users trudge to your blog. What you can do, however, is to follow a combination of smart steps to make the magic happen. Let's look at some of these measures.

Determine which Social Networks to Use

Many bloggers end up dividing scarce resources among so many sites and garner little results in the process. You can avoid the frustrations that come with this by focusing your efforts on networks selected based on sound principles.

> **6 Figure$ Tip**
> *Go to where your readers are.*

Know Where Your Target Readers Are

This seems like a no-brainer, doesn't it? But you'll be surprised at how many bloggers fall for the shiny object syndrome (don't feel bad if you've been there too) and pitch their tents everywhere and anywhere. The first rule of engagement is to know where your readers spend their time. This will mean that you must have created an ideal reader archetype which informs you of the preferences and nuances of your audience. For example, if your audience includes people who enjoy more visual content, spending so much time on LinkedIn might yield little results.

Find Out the Networks that Promise Huge Traffic

Some social media platforms can naturally send more readers your way than others. This could be due to their large followership, their compatibility with the type of content you share, or how well their set up encourages users to click on external links. Generally, the most reliable networks are Facebook, Twitter, Pinterest, Instagram, and LinkedIn. You also have social bookmarking sites like Reddit and StumbleUpon.

Ultimately, you will have to determine what works best for you by paying attention to your analytics. There you will see where the bulk of your traffic comes and get an idea of which networks serve you best.

General Questions to Ask Before Choosing Which Networks to Use

Apart from the factors discussed earlier, answering the following questions can give you a clear idea on which networks will best suit your intentions.

- What are your goals?
- What networks fit the subject of your content? Are you talking about business? Sports? Cooking? etc
- What are the most popular networks?
- What networks have the functionalities that support the promotion of external content?
- How active are your readers on social media
- What networks do your readers use?

Make Sharing Easy By Integrating Social Media with Your Blog

The beautiful thing about social media is the limitless possibilities when it comes to reach. If one of your readers with an audience reach of just 100 people shares your content, this could create a massive ripple effect that could see thousands of people view the same piece of content. The conundrum then is how to get this one person to click the share button. What better way is there to do this than to ensure that the sharing process is as seamless as possible?

Consider your readers as babies that need to be pampered and spoon-fed (in a good way, mind you). These people do not want to be stressed, and you can't blame them; they call the shots. So if you are looking to maximize their support, ensure they can conveniently share your content on social media. There are several of ways to do this, but the most common and often, more effective method is to provide social sharing buttons on your website. These buttons link directly to designated social media networks, and with one click and a log in procedure, your readers can share links and snippets of your blog post to their audience. Popular blogging systems like WordPress offer plugins you can use to put up these buttons, so no worries on that end. However, to prevent worries on another end, limit the number of buttons you provide. The whole idea is to not get readers overwhelmed with the sheer number of options available to them.

> ### 6 Figure$ Tip
> *Choose three to four networks that are most crucial to your blog and provide share buttons to them in order to direct your audience where you want them to go.*

Place a Link to Your Blog in Your Social Media profiles

When you share snippets of your blog post on social media, you could naturally decide to include a link to the full article on your blog. In such situations, you're good. But the fact is great social media usage demands that you don't flood your followers' timelines with posts riddled with links all the time. Introduce some flavor, interact with other users, and engage with their content. In such situations, people who find you interesting will most likely click on your account to view your profile. And they should find a link to your blog sitting pretty somewhere.

Re-share Older Content

Re-promote your older content on social media is another way to maximize these platforms in driving traffic to your blog. But there are filters you should send your old posts through before reposting them. The first is the time-sensitivity filter. Ensure you're not reposting time-sensitive content without proper context. Say, you wrote about something that was all the rage two years ago. You can't simply slap that back on your social media page without some reasonable context. For instance, an event that just happened could be connected to what you wrote about, it would make sense to then say something like "a throwback to when so and so happened and now this." Or perhaps you once made a prediction in an old blog post, and it has turned out to be spot on. You can link to the post as you talk about the current happenings.

There's also the success filter. With it, you'll simply be checking how well a post performed in the past to know if it's worth sharing again. If it didn't do well, then, chances are it won't garner so much attention now (there are always exceptions though, but do you really have the time to make too many gambles?).

USING DIFFERENT SOCIAL MEDIA SITES TO PROMOTE YOUR BLOG

When it comes to social media promotion, one key thing to note is that there's no one-size-fits-all hack. Different sites have varying written and unwritten rules of engagement, so you need to tailor your promotional ventures to each platform for optimal results.

> **6 Figure$ Tip**
> *Re-share your best performing evergreen content or repost old content using currently relevant context.*

Using Facebook

With 1.62 billion users visiting Facebook daily, the platform remains one of the choicest places for promotions of any type. Its wide user base, coupled with its supportive functionalities like the options of promoting blog posts on your profile, pages, and in groups, makes it irresistible for bloggers. And if it aligns with your goals, you should also leverage the platform using the following strategies.

Post Short Updates

While Facebook posts can take as much as 10,000 characters, viewers only get to see a preview that features the first 480 characters. This means the rest of your update falls behind the "see more" button. So in creating an update that links to your website, you need to get creative and wriggle within the space the 480 characters provide. It's even advisable to go lower than 480 characters since research has shown shorter posts to perform better.

Post a concise but catchy description of what's in store for the viewers when they click the link. Whet their appetite, quip about something fascinating (related to the post), but don't lie or exaggerate. Your preview should promise only what the article contains.

Use Images

Everyone loves a little visual cue, even Facebook users. That's why using images in your updates can score you more click-through points. You can go as far as uploading a full-sized image related to the blog post you are promoting. All you'll do is accompany it with a catchy headline and a link to the post. Carousel posts and GIFs aren't out of bounds too – in fact, anything relevant to the post that can pique the viewers' interest isn't!

> **6 Figure$ Tip**
> *Craft creative short previews to attract attention to your updates and get more clicks-through to your blog.*

Post Strategically for Maximum Organic Reach

It's best to post at times when you'll have the bulk of your fans online. So head on to your Page Insights and click Posts. There you will see charts showing on which days and at what hours your posts get the most views. In case you're just starting out and don't have enough data to determine your best times for posting, you can look up research-based recommendations.

The best times to post on Facebook according to Hootsuite are:

- *For the business audience: Between 9 am and 2 pm EST (Tuesday, Wednesday and Thursday)*
- *For consumer audience: 12 pm EST (Monday, Tuesday and Wednesday)*

Use Paid Ads

You might have to invest some money in ensuring that you get your updates and blog links to a particular demographic or audience. You can boost your posts or use promoted aids to reach your fans and their friends. There's also the option of targeting users based on page engagements. And it's a good one since you'll be reaching people who have once shown interest in your content.

Chirp About it on Twitter

Keep it short and Post Strategically

Twitter is also another great place to direct lots of eyeballs to your blog updates. The structure of the platform means you must keep your preview or description short and sweet. You're allowed to use up to 280 characters but keep your Tweets between 140 – 180 characters for optimal results. Don't forget to add your link.

The best times to post on Twitter according to Hootsuite are:

- *Business audience: Between 9 am and 4 pm EST (Monday or Thursday).*
- *Consumer audience: 12 pm or 1 pm EST (Monday to Wednesday).*

Drive Conversations Using Blog Excerpts

With Twitter, you can easily share bits of your blog post and drive conversations around them. For instance, if your post includes an amazing fact, share it as an excerpt via your Twitter page and ask people to share their thoughts. Somewhere during the conversations (when it feels right), you can then refer them to the full post on your blog.

Include "Click to Tweet" Links in Your Articles

Creating "click to tweet" links within your articles can also encourage visitors to your blog to share your content on Twitter. With these links, your audience can share a concise, Tweetable quote from your piece on their Twitter pages. And of course, these quotes would link back to your blog so their audience can click them and be redirected to the full article.

Add Visuals

Twitter users also love visuals, so accompany your update with appealing photos, GIFs, memes (everyone loves those), or short videos. Also, Hashtags and the @handle options are high-powered weapons you can use in your battle to be seen and heard. Ensure that your tweets always have hashtags to make them searchable (find hashtags with relevant keywords). And use the @handle feature to get the attention of specific accounts or users. However, you should only do this when your tweet relates to the handle you're tagging, or you'll risk looking like a needy baby.

> **6 Figure$ Tip**
> *Use 7-12 hashtags to promote your posts' visibility.*

Show the World on Instagram

Instagram is just perfect for promoting your blog if you deal with visual subjects like food, arts, animals, fashion, lifestyle, sports, and fitness. But don't worry, it also works for other types of blogs too. If you finally decide to hop on Instagram, here are some strategies you can use in promoting your blog:

Use Instagram Stories

Statistics show that more than 70% of Instagram users watch Instagram stories daily. This makes the feature one you must leverage if you are serious about Instagram promotions.

Using Insta stories for promoting your blog would require you to get creative. But you can borrow some ideas like spreading bits of information from your blog post on multiple story slides. Move on to wrap up the show by linking directly to your blog if the feature is available to you (you need to have at least 10k followers for this). If you do not have the feature, simply direct your followers to the link in your bio using a CTA in the final story frame. Then place the @handle sticker with your username in it so your viewers can click it and head straight to your bio.

Interact with Other Users

Another strategic way to promote your blog on Instagram is by interacting with other bloggers and influencers within your niche. Use hashtags to search for brands, influencers, bloggers, and other accounts whose interests are similar to yours and hook up with them smartly. Comment, like, and share their content. In doing so, you will catch their audience's eye, especially if you provide value through your comments.

By reaching out to these top accounts, you also open the door for future partnerships. Talk about killing two birds with a stone.

Craft Killer Captions While Posting on Your Feed

If you're using the feed, you'll be posting an image or a video. But here's the deal, you're trying to redirect your audience to your blog and possibly get them to share your post. This means your image or video needs to have some accompanying text that gives context to it, tells a story, and calls your audience to action. That's where your caption comes in.

> **6 Figure$ Tip**
> *Best Times to post, according to Hootsuite: 12 pm to 1 pm EST (Monday to Friday).*

Craft a catchy caption that revolves around the blog post. It should give your audience a taste of the content while urging them to go grab the full meal on your blog. Ask a question and answer it halfway, use shocking stats or narrate an encounter that relates to the subject of the blog post; just grab attention ethically. Don't forget to point the way to your blog by placing a link to the post in your bio and asking your audience to head there.

B. BUILDING YOUR MAILING LIST

Collating a solid mail list ranks up there with the best methods of promoting your blog and keeping readers hooked. With an ever-growing list, you can direct steady traffic to your blog regularly. This will improve your blog's reputation, increase the chances of having readers recommend or share your content, and even create earning opportunities through advertising.

Getting subscribers

The basic trick (I don't like that word) to getting people to subscribe to your newsletter is providing value upfront. You need to offer them a reason to surrender their emails. And sometimes, this reason needs to go beyond the fact that you already have great content on your website. You might need to provide more free stuff like an ebook or a helpful report. If you are dealing with your target audience and the material you've offered solves a genuine need, you'll have your mail list teeming with eager subscribers.

In addition to providing value, you need to place prompts in strategic places that will urge visitors to subscribe to your newsletter. Such prompts could include a "subscribe" button on your menu bar and a similar icon beneath your posts. There's also the option of creating timed pop-up subscription windows or forms. Ensure you include control parameters like fade time and how many times the window should show up for visitors returning in the same week. This is, so the window doesn't mar your readers' experience.

> **6 Figure$ Tip**
> *Urge visitors to provide their emails in exchange for free and valuable material.*

Now instead of simply asking them to subscribe, you could craft your message differently. If you're offering free stuff, use that as the trigger, for example: "get your *FREE* social media marketing toolkit." That's great copywriting. It takes the attention away from your desires to your viewers' needs, and so they are more eager to act.

C. USING SEARCH ENGINE OPTIMIZATION

Search engine optimization involves practices that improve the visibility of your blog on search engine results pages. By optimizing your pages for search engines, they rank highly and have a better chance of enjoying much traffic.

While many people are always agitated over the technicalities of search engine optimization, there are basic rules to follow. And chief among these rules is the creation of valuable content. People are in search of answers, so give them just that. By providing incredible value in your works, web users that stumble on your page will share them and link to them. Doing this will indicate to the search engine crawlers that your content is useful, and they'll index and ensure it ranks highly on subsequent results pages.

But of course, paying serious attention to the quality of your content doesn't stop you from complimenting your efforts with other strategies. Here are some vital ones to consider:

On-Site SEO Measures
These are practices you carry out within your blog to improve its visibility.

- Keywords: Using relevant keywords in your content can improve its visibility on search engine result pages. So while preparing content on a specific subject, research the keywords your audience will likely use in launching queries related to that topic. You can use keyword research tools like Moz Keyword Explorer, Google Keyword Planner, Ahrefs Keywords Explorer, and Soovle to find relevant options. Move on to sprinkle these keywords strategically within your article, in titles, URL, and links. However, don't go overboard because stuffing your content with keywords will only make your efforts counterproductive.

- Improve user experience so you can reduce your bounce rate: Bounce rate refers to the number of visitors who make it to your blog but leave immediately. Experts suspect that the more time people spend on websites, the more valuable Google believes the content is. And guess what the reward is? Yes, higher rankings on result pages. So to reduce your bounce rate, ensure your blog provides a great experience. We have seen the importance of content, there's also the need to consider the page loading time. And with more people viewing web pages on their mobiles, your blog needs to be optimized for such devices.
- Include ALT tags in your images. ALT tags are text descriptions that will help search engine crawlers read your image and index what it represents.
- Link to other articles within your website. This will improve the ranking of these articles and make it easier for search engine crawlers to index content on your site.

Off-Site SEO Measures

Off-site or on-page SEO involves tweaks made outside your site that affects its ranking on search engine result pages. The best off-site practices are geared towards generating backlinks (also known as inbound links) to your site. Backlinks are links to pages on your site from another website. You can consider them (because Google does) as endorsements for your websites from other sites. And the more you have, the higher your page ranks. There's a caveat, though. These votes of confidence need to come from trustworthy websites because Google "respects" their opinions. So you don't just need backlinks, you need quality ones.

Understandably, generating quality backlinks is more difficult than onsite SEO practices, but it is not impossible. Try out the following measures:

- Provide content that's way better than whatever is out there. If people find your content valuable, they'll link back to it in their own works.
- Connect with other bloggers and exchange links. To do this, you must have built some level of relationship with these people.
- Liaise with other bloggers for guest posting opportunities
- Join discussion forums and link to your blog posts
- Hop on Questions and Answers platforms like Yahoo and Quora, answer questions within your niche and link to related blog posts.
- Share your content on social media with relevant hashtags. Writers also research their topics on social sites. They can stumble upon your tweet or update on Facebook, follow the link to your blog, and reference your article in their piece.

> **6 Figure$ Tip**
> *It is not recommended to buy more than 100 backlinks every 14-30 days.*

Finally, there is another way to get backlinks that isn't as popular. That is, buying backlinks. You should know that buying backlinks is a generally risky move. You should not make it your main source of backlinks. However, if you need a boost in the number of backlinks your website has, then you could try buying backlinks.

There are several websites that you can buy backlinks from, here are some of them:

- BackLinks.com
- LinksManagement.com
- BlackHatLinks.com
- Onehourbacklinks.com

(Note: Buying backlinks is somewhat risky, so you need to ensure that the backlinks come from only high-domain authority sites. I highly recommend)

CHAPTER 4
MONETIZING YOUR BLOG

Here we are, the moment you've been waiting for. In this chapter, you'll learn a few (but very powerful) points that can help you start earning from an established blog. You'll also get to see the opportunities open to you to monetize your blog. Be aware, however, that like most good things in life, earning six figures and above will take some time. But with consistency, you can do it. Let's get right to it then.

MAKING A GOOD IMPRESSION AND MAKING YOURSELF ACCESSIBLE

The way people perceive you is everything, and this could be the difference between sealing the deal of a lifetime or missing out on it. To ensure you make the right impression, you should religiously attend to certain pages on your blog.

About Page

Your "About Me" Page gives you an opportunity to tell (and show) readers, agencies, and brands (who might be looking for advertising partners) who you are. Now it' normal to feel stumped, but knowing what you should include can get the words flowing.

- A high-resolution photo: This is about showing your human side and building a connection from the onset. Simply supply a professional-looking headshot.
- Include the basics: this includes your name and where you're based.
- Tell us why we shouldn't leave: This is where you sell yourself and get the viewers to see that you offer value. Describe yourself using your interests essentially. Then include details like what your blog is about and subtle indications of who you're writing for. With this information, the regular reader will know you can meet his needs. And advertising agencies can begin to perceive if you're a good fit for them.
- Thinking of throwing in a few examples of projects you've worked on or brands you've partnered with? By all means!

> **6 Figure$ Tip**
> *Maintain an original voice and let your personality shine through. With this, you can connect with your readers early on and give marketer's an idea of who you are.*

Partnership Page

Here, your focus turns to successful partnerships you've had and projects you've worked on. But this doesn't remove the need to also include background information on yourself, similar to what you have on the About page.

Your partnership page will serve branding and advertising agencies more than regular readers, so it's important it doesn't gloss over the details of the work you've done. Here's a summary of what it should cover:

- Some of the details on your About page including a photo of yourself, your name, interests, location, and nativity.
- A brief work history (if there's any): This helps to show agencies the range of experience you have. You never know what the specifications the campaign manager wants, so slap on anything relevant you've done or are doing.
- An iteration of services you've once offered, and you're willing to offer currently. This could include:
    - Featuring in a live Facebook video
    - Delivering sponsored blog posts, social media updates, and content forms
    - Offering sponsored ad space
    - Offering guest posting opportunities
    - Writing paid product reviews
    - Hosting events or just being at them
    - Taking the role of a contracted ambassador
    - Starring in video and photoshoots

Contact Page
Your contact page should contain information on how people can reach you. You have the option of simply supplying your email address with a short text like: "if you're a brand interested in partnering..." or you could use contact forms.

> **6 Figure$ Tip**
> *For easy sorting of mails, provide two separate emails for readers and agencies*

Ensure you have a system that allows you to sieve through emails so you can easily differentiate between emails from potential partners, regular readers, and members of the press. You can easily do this by providing two email addresses with separate instructions. Ask regular readers and other people to reach you through one and brands through the other. If you're using a contact form that links to one email, create a dropdown list that allows users to select the reason why they are reaching out. That way, you can scan through emails in your inbox and attend to the important ones first.

PRICING YOURSELF
There is no "right" amount to charge for your services, there are only reasonable price points based on what is required of you and other factors. And there are several ways to arrive at this reasonable pricing strategy, but we'll look at a few basic options you can adopt.

Pricing Based on Activity Type

Blog Posts: There is no doubt that the price you'll quote for crafting blog posts will rest largely on your reach as a blogger. Make that the first determining factor on your list. Then consider other variables like the time you'll spend in creating the content (researching, brainstorming, etc.). Also, bear in mind the resources that will go into gathering all you'll need to put out a valuable piece – will you have to journey to a particular location to gather information or interview someone? It won't also hurt to examine the likely budget the client has.

Social Media Posts: This also depends on your reach with the focus on two parameters: the number of followers you have and the average engagement your content gets. Other factors, like the requirements of the clients, will come into play too. Are they looking at video content, images, or just tweets? If yes, would you be covering the costs yourself? Would you be coming with an original concept yourself, or do the clients have a ready idea? These are some of the questions that could help you get an idea of just how much would be right to charge.

> **6 Figure$ Tip**
> *You could charge between $100 and $200 per blog post for every 10,000 pageviews. But whatever you do, be fair to yourself and show some flexibility when the need arises.*

Featuring at Events: In this case, the role you'll play at the event will be pivotal to determining your price. If all you'll do is just to be at the event, then the estimated value of your time and the transportation costs (if the client isn't covering it) should be your major parameters. However, if you'll be playing a major role, like anchoring or co-hosting the event, your price should rise.

EARNING OPPORTUNITIES

Advertising

Advertising is one of the easiest channels of earning passive income through your blog. And the added advantage is it comes in various forms, so it can be incorporated in several ways without ridding your blog of its value to readers.

Typically, bloggers use several advertising platforms, but the most popular is Google Adsense. Other similar advertising systems include BlogAds, Clickbooth, Infolinks, and Media.net.

When you've decided to include ads on your website, the next step is discovering what types are available, and the payment plans you can opt for.

Types of Ads

Banner Ads: Banner ads are graphical representations containing text, images, and links to other sites. These tools of online advertising have been around for a long time and aren't going anywhere anytime soon (even if you consider them annoying). And yes, they still convert, and that's why advertisers are ever eager to pay to have them on sites that enjoy massive traffic.

You can strike a deal to have banner ads on your blog by dealing directly with the company that wishes to place them or with a third-party ad agency like the Google Adsense.

Textual or Contextual Ads: These are very similar to banner ads except that the links to the external site aren't embedded in graphics but within the text. Here's how they work. When you sign up to have them placed on your blog, you receive ad codes that automatically embed themselves within relevant content on your blog. That way, anyone who hovers above the lines of code while reading your content gets to see a pop-up window with a link they can click. This link redirects them to the client's site, and you get paid for every click.

Types of Ad Payment
Pay-Per-Click or Cost Per Click: This system allows you to get paid based on the number of clicks the ads on your blog get. You are paid per click.

Cost Per Action (CPA): Here, you only get paid when the visitor takes a definite action apart from clicking the link. Such actions could include making a purchase, signing up for a class, or subscribing to a newsletter.

Cost Per Thousand Views (CPM): You receive a fixed amount for the number of times an ad is displayed on your blog.

> **6 Figure$ Tip**
> *Textual ads are great since they don't deface your blog like banner ads.*

Getting Advertisers
Apart from dealing with Ad platforms like Google Adsense, you can contact businesses directly and ask to host their ads on your blog. Here's how to do that.

- Begin by putting together a concise brochure you can use to pitch to advertisers. This document should contain details like the latest viewership stats, including information on viewer demographics, your rates, available offers, and contact details. If you have references or testimonials, there's no harm in slipping some in too.
- Reach out to companies that might be interested in placing ads on blogs so they can deal with you directly. You need to ensure you have a viable list of prospects before launching out. For instance, your list should mostly include companies within your niche who have always placed ads on blogs.

    Once you have your list, begin to shoot the companies emails detailing who you are and why you're reaching out. Sell yourself and show why you're a good fit for them. Don't forget to include your brochure too. Above all, keep your pitch short and sweet.

Affiliate Marketing
Affiliate marketing involves receiving a commission for referring a customer to a client's product. When signing up to become an affiliate marketer, you receive a customized link that

redirects customers to a product. For every visitor that clicks that link on your site and purchases the product, you get a referral bonus. Popular platforms that offer this opportunity include the ninety-pound gorilla: Amazon, LinkShare, Shareasale, and Commission Junction. A simple registration procedure will get you into any of these platforms' affiliate programs.

While hopping on the affiliate marketing bandwagon isn't difficult, you need to note some things to make it work.

- Be careful not to mislead your readers or recommend a subpar product. This means you'll need to research a product before asking your viewers to check it out. It's also important you express your honest views, including doubts, should there be any.
- Ensure links are placed within matching content. Links embedded in related pieces of content have been found to perform better than those placed randomly.
- Do it for your audience. Naturally, you create content your audience wants, and that's why they keep coming back. It's why they love your blog. In the same vein, you should only link to products your readers would want, and you'd increase their chances of making a purchase. So don't neglect what you already know about your audience while choosing products to feature or review.

> **6 Figure$ Tip**
> *Do not wait for companies or advertising agencies to come to you, go to them.*

Products and Subscriptions

Apart from linking to other people's products, you can create yours too. It's good to give your viewers value for free, but you can also offer your knowledge or expertise for cash. All you have to do is draw the line to separate what goes for free and what goes for a fee. Once you're ready, identify a major need in your niche and create materials you can give to your audience at a reasonable price. Examples of such products include:

- Ebooks and other downloadable documents like PDF workbooks and templates
- Full courses
- Audio materials
- Video materials
- Live webinars or tutorials

What's more, you can also offer special membership areas for a subscription fee. Say you're a certified emotional intelligence coach. Some of your materials and tips will be accessible for free, but you can create a special club where members get unfettered access to you. You could also share bits of content in public while you give the entire package to paying subscribers.

Sponsored Blog Posts

When you create a sponsored post, you get paid for writing about something. This could be an event, a product, a service, or any other subject. In such situations, you would either work with a company directly or a branding agency handling an organization's campaign.

Seize opportunities for writing sponsored posts by positioning yourself strategically. Follow companies within your niche and be on hand to send a proposal when they are launching a campaign you think you can promote with a post. There's no harm in asking to write or talk about their upcoming product launch too.

You can also hook up with branding agencies and influencer networks. Influencer networks are digital marketplaces where bloggers can view brands' upcoming campaigns and send in proposals. They are super plugs for sponsored gigs. A few of them you can look at are Cohley, Izea, Tapinfluence, Collectively, AspireQ, and She Speaks.

Whether you're partnering with brands or third-party agencies, you'll need to have a brochure you can present. Some parts of the brochure could remain fixed, like your blog stats and viewers' demographics. But you might need to construct custom messages that show why you are a good fit for that particular promotional post or campaign.

Other Earning Opportunities

An easy way to hit six-figure income even in your early days as a blogger is by combining the direct methods of earning from your blog with fringe earning avenues or side gigs. These options can be very lucrative, too, and can complement whatever you bag from blogging.

> **6 Figure$ Tip**
>
> *Offer free value consistently and your audience will be willing to pay a price for some extra value… Do not put yourself in a box, rather, open yourself up to different earning opportunities and grow your income.*

Freelancing

There's no harm in taking on the task of writing for other people's blogs on the side. It pays well (if you know your onions) and gives you the opportunity to sharpen your skills while receiving remuneration. Not to mention that it helps you connect with other bloggers and influencers in ways that could open up bigger future opportunities.

If you want to get snapped up for such gigs, then you'll need to take your blog seriously, as this helps to demonstrate your expertise. So write and create content to also showcase your skills.

You should also get the word out that you're in the market for blogging gigs. Place notifications on your blog and social media profiles. Do well to relate with other bloggers and share your content on various platforms to promote visibility. Finally, get yourself on freelancing platforms like freelancewritinggigs.com, jobs.problogger.net, and several others.

Speaking
Getting paid speaking engagements will take a while, especially if you're yet to establish yourself as an authority in your niche. Latching on to such opportunities will also prove difficult if you aren't writing on certain topics. But accomplished bloggers in relevant niches can snag such openings easily. So, build your blog's reputation and keep an eye out for speaking engagements.

Offering Additional Services
- Graphics design
- Web design
- Social media management
- Editing and proofreading

CONCLUSION

There you have it: a blueprint to guide your expedition into the blogging world. Refuse to be held down by analysis paralysis. *"A journey of a thousand miles begins with a single step"* Lao Tzu said. Many people read books. But fewer people act with the knowledge that they have accumulated. Rather than chose to be one of the *misfits* that change the world, they become huge banks and storehouses of data- talking about the change that's happening in the world around them. Which group are you going to number with: The group of people who actually participate in the development of our cosmos or those that merely chant it? Remember, it isn't ideas that change the world; it's executed ideas. Ready? Set? Execute!

www.ingramcontent.com/pod-product-compliance
Lightning Source LLC
Chambersburg PA
CBHW081100240526
45465CB00025B/2791